The Rebel Spoonie Manifesto

Disclaimer:
This book is not intended as a substitute for the medical or psychological advice of physicians or therapists. The reader should consult a therapist or physician in matters relating to the reader's health and particularly with respect to any symptoms that may require diagnosis or medical or psychological attention.

Copyright @ 2023 Christina Buckner Foster

All rights reserved. No part of this book may be reproduced or used in any manner without the prior written permission of the copyright owner, except for the use of brief quotations in a book review.

To request permissions, contact the publisher at rebelspooniemanifesto@gmail.com

table of contents

The Rebel Spoonie Manifesto
-about this workbook -definitions

-why we need a rebel spoonie manifesto

Rebuild
-may I introduce you to YOU? -10 truths about me

Solidify
-love your inner kiddo -shrine of love & protection

-the damage of negative self talk

Rebel
-the power of rebellion -our bodies -our boundaries

Create
-our creativity

Unite
-our community -asking for help

Create your own Rebel Spoonie Manifesto

special features

Rebel Spoonie Shift
-in these sections you will be shown a different perspective and asked to consider a new viewpoint

Questions to Consider
-these questions are designed to help you dive deeper into each topic

Collages
-more about the collages under "our creativity"

for Theo & Kai

for June

for all my brilliant friends

thank you Theo & Emily
for supporting me in making
this book a reality

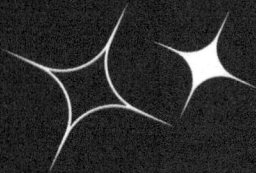

about this workbook

The Rebel Spoonie Manifesto Workbook is designed to be used individually or in a group. For a deeper dive, connect with a life coach, therapist, or person you really trust.

The Rebel Spoonie Manifesto Workbook can be given to friends, families, loved ones and professionals to help them get a better understanding of what we go through.

I highly encourage you to take your time with this book. There is no end date to any of these actions or perspective shifts. Use them and change them as they fit. The goal is you being able to live your most authentic and fullfilling life despite chronic health issues.

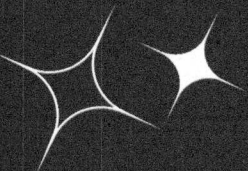

about this workbook

There are situations where the content in this workbook may not be suitable. For example, if you are in a domestic violence situation, setting boundaries can be dangerous. Please make sure you are getting the appropriate professional help to keep yourself safe and use your own discretion.

The information in this workbook is also designed to be a starting point and not an end all. Due to the shortened length, there are many issues I was not able to delve into.

Please know that I have tried to be as aware as possible that every one of us has different strengths and limitations within ourselves and in our environments. Please adjust any of the content in this book to work for you.

Dear Rebel Spoonies,

This is not a process with an end goal

This is a journey

You will mess up

You will ebb and flow

You will stumble

However you will learn to have compassion and grace for yourself when you do. You will remind yourself you are new at this and new things simply take practice and time

I believe in you!!!

Christina

Spoonie

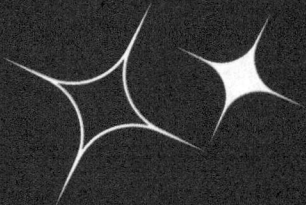

A label used by those with chronic health issues originating from chronic illness blogger Christine Miserandino using spoons as a metric to explain the energy levels of people with chronic health conditions. Every person has a set amount of spoons (energy) to use for tasks to get through each day. People with chronic illnesses have fewer spoons to work with.

Rebel

someone who acts in disobedience or shows opposition

Manifesto

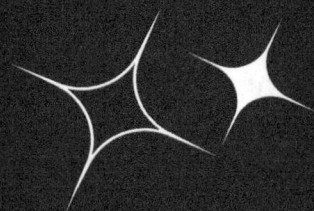

a written statement declaring publicly the intentions, motives, or views of its issuer

Rebel Spoonie

Those with chronic health issues who refuse to live by the ideology created by those who are healthy. We refuse to meet impossible standards. We are the experts on ourselves.

Rebel Spoonie Manifesto

We rebel against the thought pain and happiness cannot coexist

We rebel against the notion that our illnesses equate our worth

We rebel against the idea we need to look sick as proof of being sick

We rebel against the ableist and oppressive systems of this society

We are taking back our power

We are rewriting the rules

The Rebel Spoonie Manifesto is our guidebook

The Rebel Spoonie Manifesto Workbook is step one to creating that guidebook

why we need a rebel spoonie manifesto

Both spoken and unspoken cultural rules for people who suffer with chronic health issues were formed by people who have only ever experienced temporary ailments. Not only does the destructiveness of this derivative archetype cause unnecessarily damage due to misguided advice, ableism, and internalized shame, it also robs the world of the offerings of countless brilliant minds and compassionate souls.

Living in a society that hinges on the verge of collapse without able-bodied and able-minded individuals has generated a cult-like level of toxic productivity that leaves those who cannot meet production standards feeling worthless and encourages those who are able to demand proof from those who claim they are ill.

How do you escape a cult?

You Rebel!!!

- You get real with yourself
- You educate yourself
- You find your people
- You create community
- You build each other up
- You challenge the system
- You rewrite the rules
- You live authentically

Rebuild

may I introduce you to YOU!

Most every spoonie will tell you one of the most difficult problems when dealing with persistent health issues has nothing to do with the physical and everything to do with the mental and emotional.

Chronic illness strips away a person's identity at differing levels depending upon the severity of the disease. Spend any time at all in the spoonie community and you will encounter this phrase repeatedly - "I don't even recognize myself."

You find yourself looking through old photos wondering, "Who was that person? Smiling and laughing?" The photos almost mock the person returning the stare in the mirror.

may I introduce you to YOU!

"Who am I?"

this is where we begin

10 truths about me

From the moment the air from this world hits our skin, the programming of this realm begins. A loved one mentions they love you in the color periwinkle, so it becomes your favorite color. A unicorn charm given to you by your favorite teacher in elementary school becomes your lifelong aesthetic. I'm sure you can think of many examples from your own life that evoke a sense of comfort and nostalgia.

Not so comfortable or nostalgic are the billions and billions of dollars each year spent in marketing and advertising to tell us over and over who we are, what we want, and why we are so broken that such and such product is the only thing that could ever make us whole again.

Who are you when all of that is stripped away?

Who are you without the input of your partner, parents, siblings, kid, priest or teacher?

10 truths about me

Most people struggle with these questions simply because we have never needed to ask them of ourselves. However, when chronic pain and illness has stolen parts of your identity, these questions become the difference between merely existing and thriving. I mean how can someone even enjoy life if they don't even truly know what they enjoy?

For spoonies having truths about ourselves helps to combat the vulnerability and struggles we face. For example, if someone claims you are exaggerating your condition and you know for a fact that you value truth, combating their gaslighting becomes a much easier task.

The following exercise is to help rebuild your foundation and call back your wonderful self.

Throughout the course of the workbook you will discover how these 10 Truths will strengthen you again and again.

10 Truths About Me
(example)

- I am honest
- I am creative
- I am loving
- I give grace
- I am peaceful

- I am persistent
- I am thoughtful
- I am smart
- I am resourceful
- I am joyful

10 Truths About Me

Directions

Write down 10 truths about yourself. These truths must only come from you with as little influence from others as possible. If you need to ask others for input, ask yourself if their input resonates with your personal truth. When you are finished, do what you need to do to commit your 10 truths to memory.

10 Truths About Me

10 Truths About Me

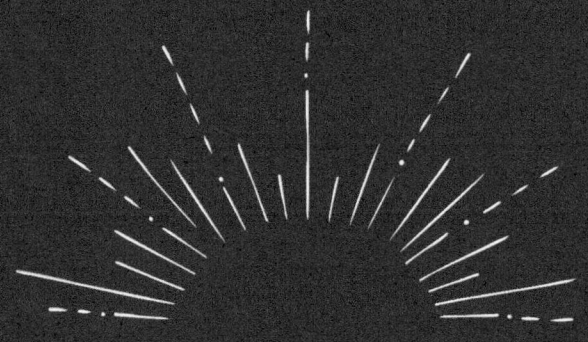

question to consider

Have you become unintentionally typecast in a role that was written by healthy members of our society who have never had to deal with chronic health issues?

write it out

write it out

write it out

Solidify

love your inner kiddo

We all have parts of ourselves that we have deemed utterly unlovable and irretrievably damaged.

If society hasn't already kicked us in the ass with negative experiences, struggling with chronic health issues will dropkick you straight in the boxing ring with the toughest and most unpredictable of foes.

Body size and shape changes, tooth and hair loss, loss of the ability to think or speak are just a few issues that can occur with ongoing illnesses.

Self-esteem? TKO

shrine of love & protection

Directions:

- Find a location you pass multiple times per day. This could be a dresser, a counter, a table. Place your picture (or similar item) on this spot. Surround the picture with the rest of the items you gathered

- Every time you pass your little shrine, give yourself the love you deserved and deserve. Tell that little girl she is worthy of all of the love and attention in the universe. Tell that kiddo version of you their desires were valid and reasonable. Tell that boy version of you he deserved more hugs. Do this until you feel that version of yourself is lovable once again.

- Repeat with older versions of yourself until you meet and love your current self

write it out

write it out

write it out

the damage of negative self-talk

Recently I went through an awful season. Prior toxicity I had allowed in my life had left me with little to no self-esteem. During that time, I decided to place a boundary of self-love that I would no longer allow people to say mean things to me (and I got to decide what felt mean). Holding this boundary with others served to strongly highlight my own self-talk.

"How can you hold people to a standard you won't even apply to yourself?

"What good does it do to keep others from speaking mean to you if you take over their job?"

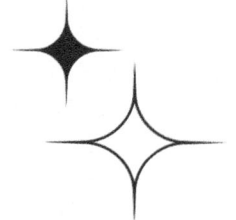

the damage of negative self-talk

According to Chief Wilma Mankiller "Negative thoughts were treated by Cherokee healers with the same medicines as wounds, headaches, or physical illness. It was believed that unchecked negative thoughts can permeate the being and manifest themselves in negative actions."

The decision to cease speaking negatively about myself was solidified when I caught myself calling myself stupid (among other things) when editing videos of me singing and playing guitar. I suddenly felt very sorry for that woman on the other end of the screen.

What had she done to deserve such vitriol?

the damage of negative self-talk

I'm not much of a slow roll type of person. Once I have decided to do something I have usually investigated every forgotten corner and developed a fifty-page business model. Often we overthink as passive noncommittal.

However, sometimes new habits can form quickly and easily. When our brain connects just how beneficial these practices are, we don't need a thirty-two step program, a shake and therapy appointments to commit.

I am not saying the process will always be easy. But most things in life that are worth anything are worth fighting for

What has occurred since I stopped the negative self-talk?

the damage of negative self-talk

Besides simply being happier and life being more peaceful...

my creativity has skyrocketed because my brain has extra space and is welcoming of new and unique thoughts instead of being judgmental. Think of being surrounded by a group of people who always tear down your work. Would you want to produce more for them to bash?

I realized all these negative tapes that were playing were causing me to miss out on so much beauty and love.

the damage of negative self-talk

I noticed making decisions that were good for myself became incredibly easy. I no longer beat myself up when I do something not so great for myself that ends in a natural reaction beyond my control.

I easily listen to my physical and emotional needs over that of fulfilling short lived desires.

I also began to refuse to allow people around me to speak negatively about themselves. This has resulted in stronger, deeper, and more authentic relationships.

I even refuse to engage in social media where someone is degrading themselves. I'm saddened when people say mean things about themselves just like I was saddened when I saw myself doing the same while editing videos.

write it out

write it out

write it out

Rebel Spoonie Shift

As people who regularly deal with extreme negativity from the world due to physical or mental health issues beyond our control, speaking negatively to ourselves is simply a luxury we cannot afford

Commit to refusing to allow negative self-talk permanently

questions to consider

- How do you speak to yourself?

- Do you speak to yourself with kindness and compassion? If not, why not?

- If you witnessed a loved one being treated with the same self talk you use, how would you feel?

- How much of your self talk is actually yours?

- How much of your self talk comes from outside sources?

- Can you think of ways your self talk helps you?

- Can you think of ways your self talk hurts you?

write it out

write it out

write it out

Rebel

LIKE WILMA MANKILLER SAID

the power
of rebellion

I have always found a particular power in rebellion. I grew up on the wrong side of pretty much everything. I was poor, brown, raised Jehovah's Witness until I was thirteen, raised by my grandparents. My very existence was an act of rebellion. I learned early on letting the pressure and influence of others who didn't have my best interest at heart dictate my actions was participating in my own oppression. That pissed me right off.

Again, who does each thought or idea benefit?

If a thought doesn't benefit me, who does it benefit and what are the applicable motives?

The answer to these questions helps me decide whether it's time for me to learn from an outside source OR dig deeper into my own truths and understandings.

The latter is often seen as rebellion.

the power of rebellion

I see striving to understand myself deeper and standing in my authenticity as nothing less than empowering. We should be at least as willing to learn and glean from our internal voices as we are those of others. I would argue more. The key to growth is being open to both.

**Let's look at this concept from a
more macro perspective**

How could we, as spoonies, ever understand our true power as a united front if we haven't even begun to tap into our own power individually?

our bodies

When we feel our worst our bodies are fighting hard to make us better. The body is brilliant. Often when one system is struggling or something is wrong, our bodies go into action mode with plans B through Z. Unfortunately, any plan other than plan A is going to feel increasingly uncomfortable.

We can be so harsh on our bodies for shrinking and expanding and simply doing their jobs. Side note: if humans were meant to stay the same size forever our skin wouldn't have the capability of stretching.

You didn't think the negative self-talk would end with your body, did you? Instead of getting angry or frustrated at your body about the very real and valid symptoms you are experiencing, try thanking your body for fighting for you. Our bodies deserve love too.

Rebel Spoonie Shift

Commit to hyping your body up permanently

write it out

write it out

write it out

our boundaries

- Due to the inherent vulnerability of those of us who deal with chronic health situations, learning how to set good boundaries is paramount to thriving.

- Boundaries are for the person setting them.

- Boundaries are not threats.

- Boundaries are what we will do if someone doesn't respect our wishes.

- Boundaries are not trying to force someone else to respect our wishes.

- Boundaries are not always safe to set verbally. Sometimes they are only for ourselves to know. Only you know your environment. Stay safe.

hey i really don't like
it when you do said
thing. So if you
continue doing said
thing I will react by
doing my own said
thing

                                        does said thing

no hard feelings but
now i gotta do my
own said thing

                                              ...

does own said thing
lives happily ever after

questions to consider

- What boundaries would you like to set in your life?

- What action will you take if those boundaries are broken?

- Can you set those boundaries with compassion and grace for the other party and yourself?

- Can you take action if a boundary is broken with compassion and grace for yourself and the other party?

write it out

write it out

write it out

Rebel Spoonie Shift

Commit to loving yourself by learning to set better boundaries

write it out

write it out

write it out

Create

Rebel Spoonie Shift

start every day with this question

How am I creating today?

When asking yourself this question try to have two perspectives in mind

- What art are you creating today?

- What type of day are you creating?

write it out

write it out

write it out

our creativity

In designing this workbook, I knew I wanted creativity to be a central aspect. In my own journey, I have found visual art to be incredibly supportive. When I'm in too much pain to play guitar or when my brain is too foggy to write, visual art allows my thoughts to venture elsewhere for a while.

The collages within this book are an example of just that – me using times when my body and mind aren't up for other types of creativity to allow my brain to explore through visual art.

Each collage is personal to me and my experience. Every choice was intentional, often even including the name of the font. As someone in a constant battle with perfectionism, I decided to allow myself space to create without judgment.

our creativity

When I look at the collages that I designed to help me heal, I feel a small sense of closure. When I look at those collages I created to mark a victory, I feel a sense of celebration.

Creativity is an incredibly powerful tool for dealing with the day-to-day battles brought by chronic conditions.

Some people say they aren't creative. However, I believe everyone is creative in some way. There is a strong likelihood if someone doesn't believe they are creative, they simply haven't found their creative expression yet.

Being spoonies can also make the act of being creative challenging in several ways. Not only do we have less bandwidth physically and mentally than normies (those without chronic health challenges), any extra activity can easily deplete us for days or longer.

our creativity

On top of that many of us have very real and valid grief from having to let go of passions our bodies used to be able to pursue. As a musician, this is very real for me. I have had to give up performing on stage for nearly a decade at this point. A long time ago I decided I would strengthen whatever areas of musicianship I could while I was fighting for my health to improve enough to return to the stage.

During that time, I clocked countless hours on the guitar, singing, and songwriting. I learned how to self-record and produce. I did all I could to learn the business aspects of music. I was too sick to perform full songs. But I could manage a thirty second video for social media.

our creativity

Please do not see the purpose of me telling you how I used my time as bragging. The purpose of me telling you how I used my time is to show you there are many steps between nothing and the stage just as there are many steps between nothing and whatever your passion was or is.

Each of those steps is incredibly important and can be purposeful and bring great joy and fulfillment. In fact, the skills you learn and the knowledge you gain could take you to even greater opportunities than you could ever have imagined.

One heavyweight key to happiness is to realize you are going to need to be flexible when challenges come, healthy or not. All or nothing mentalities hurt us. All or nothing mentalities also hurt others because we withhold the gifts we could bring.

our creativity

If we can't run, maybe we can walk. If we can't walk, maybe we can dance in our seats. If we can't stand up and play guitar on stage, maybe we find a kickass chair to sit in and play.

If you allow yourself to create and have fun without self-judgement or self-criticism, you have given yourself the gift of being able to be free to be the you that you used to know.

Sometimes most or all of our passions are truly stripped away. Please don't take me as dismissive. I want to affirm your experience. There's no need to candy coat what we go through. I'm truly sorry if this is your experience in any way. I hope some other info in these pages will be of help somehow.

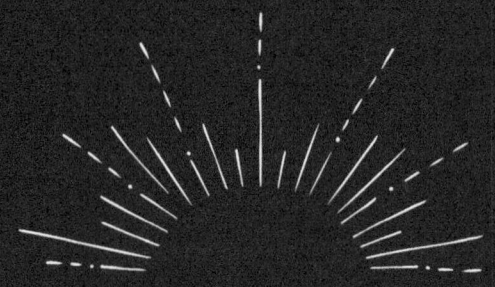

questions to consider

- What is a passion you completely gave up on due to your condition?

- What are some ways you can still enjoy that passion?

- Make a list of all of the steps between nothing and your passion.

write it out

write it out

write it out

Unite

our community

The isolation and vulnerability that come along with chronic health conditions are often more dangerous than the conditions themselves.

We are not powerless to change this!

In fact the spoonie community is vast and immensely supportive!

our community

Often as spoonies we feel as invisible as our illnesses. Having to continually focus so intensely on your own health needs in order to survive tends to limit your contact with the outside world. Out of sight out of mind really does apply in this context. We often become small and feel like our voices are powerless.

We've been taught our worth through a lens that benefits capitalism. We've been taught all or nothing, go big or go home, no pain no gain.

We've been taught if we cannot give our 100% at all times then we are worthless.

our community

We've been taught that a simple text to a friend who is struggling would never even matter. I cannot tell you how wrong you would be if you believe that. I know far too many who hang on one simple "checking in on you" text per day.

If you're struggling yourself and can't handle a full-on conversation, you can always preface the text with something like "Hey, low on spoons here but I wanted you to know you're loved."

When I was in college an elderly man taught me a lesson I will never forget. Being the introvert that I am, I would often park to study and eat my lunch in my car. I am also a creature of habit, so for a semester I found myself parking in front of a serene, wooded area many used for walking. I hadn't been there much before I had seen the same older gentleman walking the path daily at the same time. I noticed he walked slowly and with his head down. Not like someone with a purpose.

our community

Rather, like someone who was just carrying his body around. Something nudged me to wave hello.

Let me tell you I definitely resisted. I had a number of excuses to not wave. However, out of all the excuses that held me back from waving to this man, the excuse that held me back for days was "A wave won't matter. It's just a wave."

Then one day after the nudge wouldn't leave me alone, I had the thought "If it's just a wave and it won't matter, then why is waving to this man such a big deal to me?"

And thus began an entire semester of me waving at him and him kindly waving back at me.

He never approached me and I never approached him. Just waved from a distance. One day that changed. Instead of his normal wave, he gently approached my car.

our community

He then told me, "I know the school year is about to wrap up and before the semester ends and I never see you again, I want to tell you that your wave got me out of my house every day."

He didn't elaborate. Said he didn't want to take my time.

I don't know what his story was. I don't even know his name.

I do know he taught me to never dismiss the power of a small gesture of connection with another human

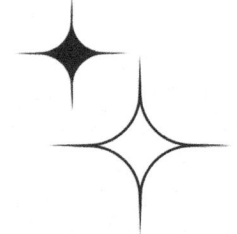

Rebel Spoonie Shift

Realize that in order to fully show up for others you must step into your own beauty and truth. Not society's version of your beauty and truth. Your OWN version of your beauty and truth. Part of that truth is accepting your own worthiness and taking up that space.

Understand you are important and needed in this world as is and every gift you bring has the power to change the world

a few building community ideas

- Text a spoonie friend
    - offer encouragement
    - send a funny meme
    - celebrate small achievements

- Set up a call with a spoonie friend

- Leave a special post for a spoonie friend on social media

- Join a group online or in person. There are groups for just about every condition. (We would love and celebrate you in the *Rebel Spoonie Manifesto* Facebook group as well!)

- Set up a video call with a spoonie friend

- Meet a spoonie friend for coffee

- Mail a spoonie friend a care package or a letter

- Take a class with a spoonie friend either online or in person

write it out

write it out

write it out

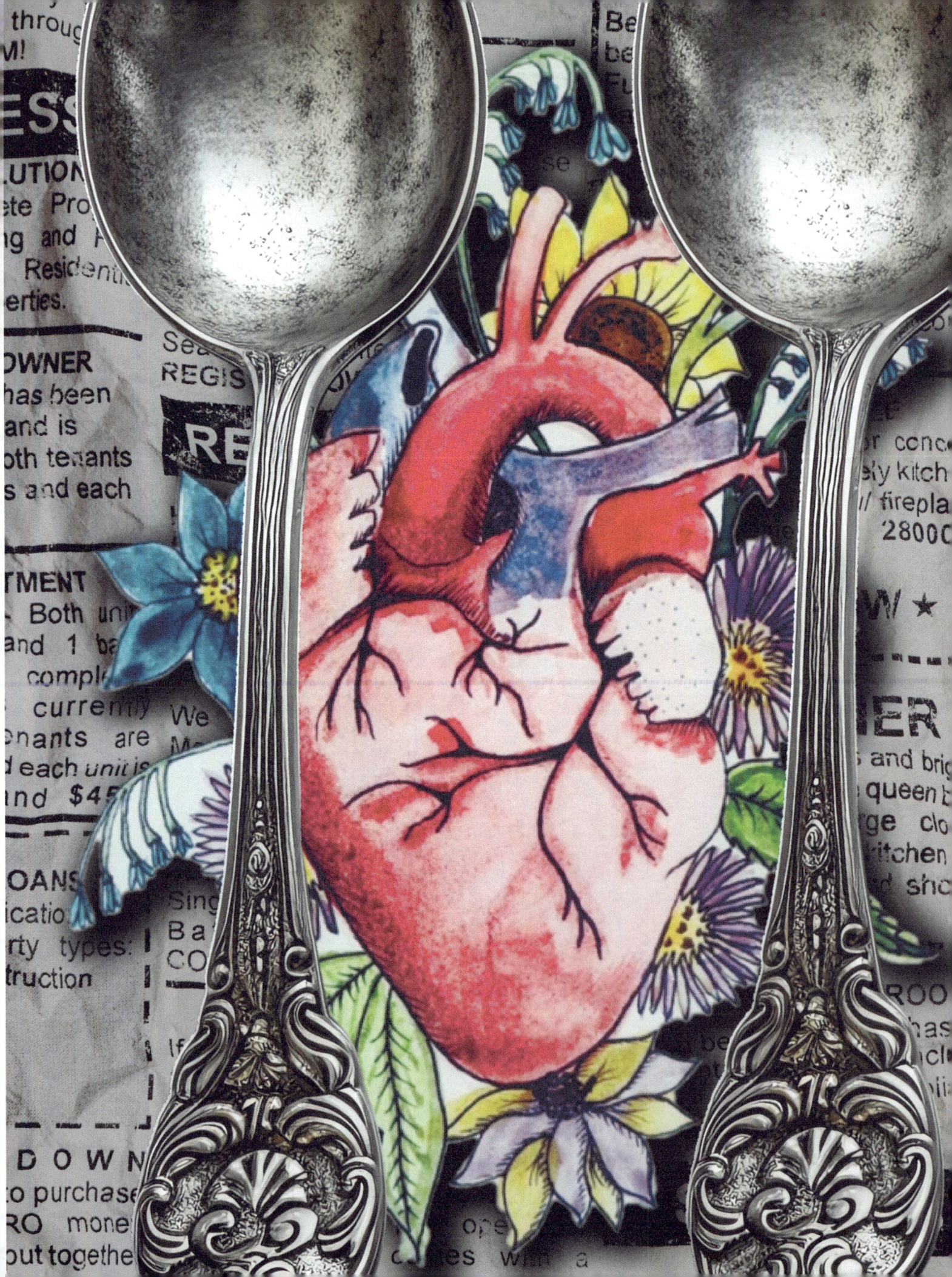

asking for help

We live in a society that considers needing help a weakness and asking for help a character defect.

Many of us are taught to be proud of the fact that we don't ask for help. Rugged individualism is woven throughout the fabric of colonialism and benefits capitalism by separating the community.

In a close knit community there is no need to pay for babysitters or caregivers.

I often think of my Cherokee ancestors and wonder if they had to ask for help in the ways that we do. Or, if they took care of each other by looking out for the needs of one another preemptively.

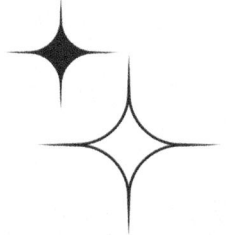

asking for help

Any issue that negatively affects society as a whole impacts those of us with chronic health conditions much more intensely and directly.

Societal judgement and disdain for those who are in legitimate need of help is one of the major hurdles to actually asking for and getting support.

Here's the deal, we aren't going to play by rules that hurt us any longer.

Asking for help when you need it is key to surviving and thriving. It takes practice and is never easy, but asking for help is **STRENGTH**!

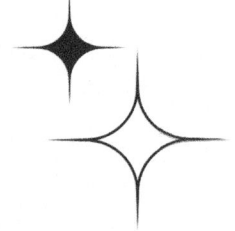

ideas when asking for help

KNOW exactly what you need. Don't expect others to figure it out for you. Only you know your life.

Realize that the answer may be no and be ready and okay to accept that answer. You getting help is your responsibility.

Realize the answer may be yes, but not in the way you want. Be willing to compromise.

Try not not feel rejected. Remember everyone has their own struggles. Ask yourself if you asked a safe person.

Have backup plans in case the answer is no.

Only ask reliable people.

Only ask safe people for help. Some people will be safe for some asks and some for others.

If you cannot find help in people reach out to organizations

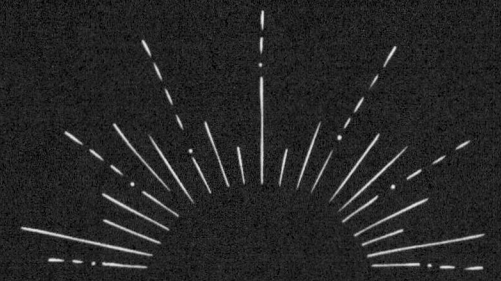

questions to consider

- Who does it benefit for you to not ask for help?

- Where did you get the idea asking for help was bad?

- Are there people you are depriving of opportunities to learn and grow by asking them for help?

- How much better would your life be if you were able to ask for the help you need?

write it out

write it out

write it out

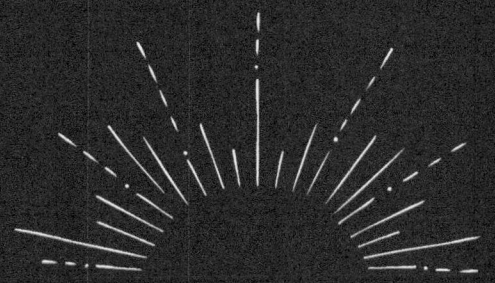

questions to consider

- What positive aspects has having a chronic illness forged within you?

- How has having a chronic condition changed you for the better?

- How can you celebrate these new and positive characteristics within yourself? (You earned it!)

write it out

write it out

write it out

Rebel Spoonie Manifesto

We rebel against the thought pain and happiness cannot coexist

We rebel against the notion that our illnesses equate our worth

We rebel against the idea we need to look sick as proof of being sick

We rebel against the ableist and oppressive systems of this society

We are taking back our power

We are rewriting the rules

The Rebel Spoonie Manifesto is our guidebook

The Rebel Spoonie Manifesto Workbook is step one to creating that guidebook

Create your own Rebel Spoonie Manifesto

Directions

Use the following pages to create your own personal Rebel Spoonie Manifesto using what you've learned about yourself throughout the process of this workbook.

Rebel Spoonie Manifesto

Rebel Spoonie Manifesto

Rebel Spoonie Manifesto

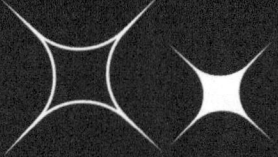

The future of the Rebel Spoonie Manifesto

As French philosopher Albert Camus so eloquently stated, "Every rebellion implies some kind of unity." If we want to make our lives better as people with chronic health conditions, we must find a better way to unite.

The future of the Rebel Spoonie Manifesto is defining the culture of spoonies, uniting forces to support, protect and empower one another, and ultimately rewrite the rules by owning our brilliance!

author bio

christina buckner foster

is a life coach, musician, and rebel spoonie known for breaking down erroneous paradigms in order to rebuild optimal lives.

Her unique life story, writings, and music have been featured in national media.

Her song FLARE reverberated through the chronic illness community as an anthem demonstrating being powerful while in pain.

With a remarkable journey that includes dealing with multiple chronic conditions, being mixed ethnically, experiencing extreme poverty, being raised in a cult, and even joining a rock band at 40, Christina's distinctive perspectives allow her to cut through the superfluous with compassion, humor, and precision. In other words, she has had to learn to rebel against certain systems in order to thrive.

Her passion is derived from the knowledge that when people are given what they need to make survival easier, thriving is inevitable. Realizing the power behind the message that you indeed can live a happy and satisfying life alongside pain and misery, Christina decided it was time to begin The Rebel Spoonie Manifesto journey with The Rebel Spoonie Manifesto Workbook

Made in the USA
Coppell, TX
13 March 2024